BRITAIN'S HERITAGE
Town Halls

Karen Averby

I gratefully acknowledge and wholeheartedly thank everyone who has granted permission to include their images in this book, and to the organisations who have kindly permitted copyright material to be reproduced, with special mention to Abigail Garrad of Wirral Libraries/ Wirral Council, Will Meredith of Wirral Archives Service, Laura Steele of Skipton Town Hall/ Craven District Council, Essex Record Office, and Luci Gosling of Mary Evans Picture Library. Uttermost thanks are also due to Nick Wright, Michelle Doig, James Wright, Carol Cragoe, and last but not least, to Jay Garrett. Every effort has been made to trace copyright holders and to obtain their permission for the use of copyright material. If copyright material has been inadvertently used without permission/ acknowledgement, then the necessary corrections will be made at the earliest opportunity.

First published 2022

Amberley Publishing
The Hill, Stroud
Gloucestershire, GL5 4EP

www.amberley-books.com

Copyright © Karen Averby, 2022

The right of Karen Averby to be identified as the Author of this work has been asserted in accordance with the Copyrights, Designs and Patents Act 1988.

ISBN 978 1 4456 8810 7 (paperback)
ISBN 978 1 4456 8811 4 (ebook)

All rights reserved. No part of this book may be reprinted or reproduced or utilised in any form or by any electronic, mechanical or other means, now known or hereafter invented, including photocopying and recording, or in any information storage or retrieval system, without the permission in writing from the Publishers.

British Library Cataloguing in Publication Data.
A catalogue record for this book is available from the British Library.

Typesetting by SJmagic DESIGN SERVICES, India.
Printed in the UK.

Contents

	Introduction	4
1	Eighteenth Century	15
2	Nineteenth Century	23
3	Twentieth Century	33
4	Twenty-first Century	44
5	Town Halls and Society	51
	What Next?	63

Introduction

Town halls in towns and cities throughout the country are the physical embodiment of local democracy, and urban expressions of local civic pride. They reflect the character and urban pride of the town or city in which they were built, and despite variations in ages and forms, it is their function as symbolic civic and public buildings housing all municipal functions that unites them.

As places of local governance they are where policy meetings and debates are held, and decisions on local issues are made. They house mayoral and council chambers, committee rooms, spaces for large public meetings, and a swathe of departments concerned with all aspects of municipal administration that serves the local population, from council tax to refuse collection, and parking permits to planning. They traditionally dominate a central location within towns

The magnificent Grade I listed Gothic-baroque Leeds Town Hall was built between 1853 and 1858 and altered in 1877. It was designed by the then little-known architect Cuthbert Brodrick, later known as 'master of the grandiose'. (Author's collection)

Introduction

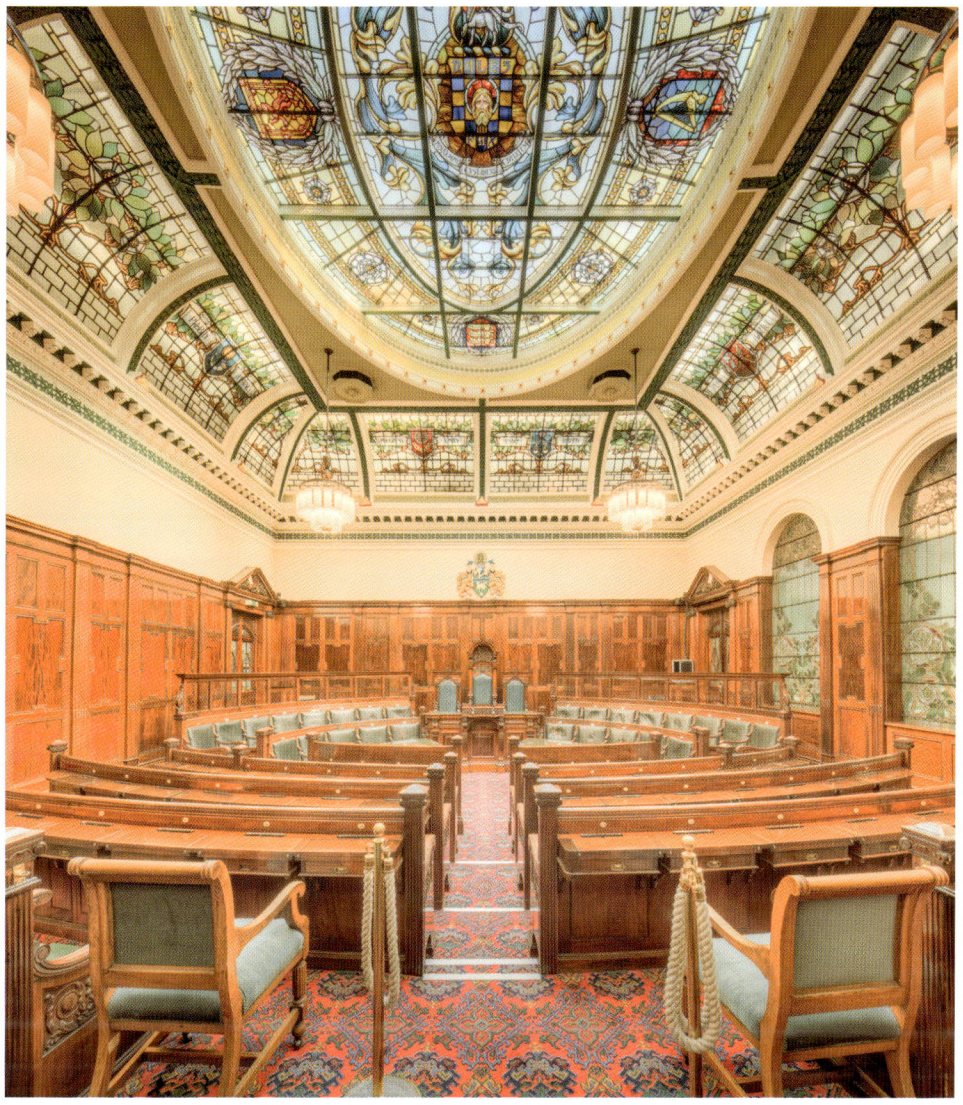

Council Chamber, Halifax Town Hall. (Michael D. Beckwith)

and cities, often next to an associated central formalised public space, and vary greatly in form and size, from the magnificently mighty Manchester and Leeds town halls to the more modest former town hall building at Corfe Castle, and everything in between.

The highly sophisticated system of local governance we see today developed over centuries, housed in buildings constructed in response to changing needs in society and in local government, while reflecting national trends in economic, social, political history. The size, form and date of these buildings were largely dependent upon the development and requirements of the town and community in which they were built to serve.

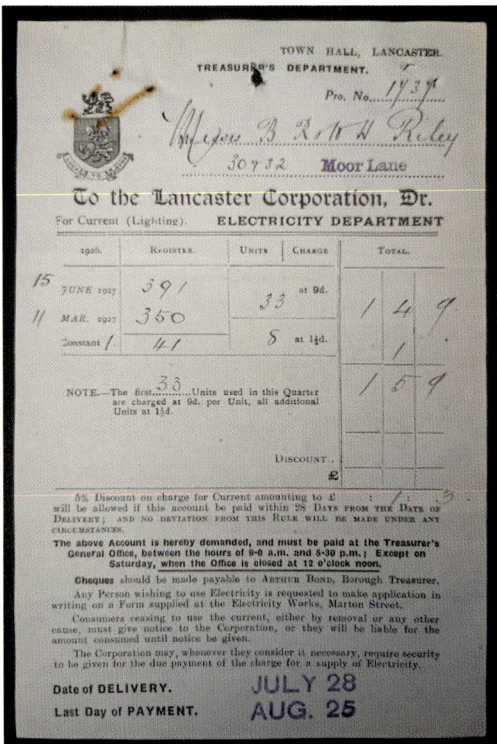

The origins of the town hall can be traced from the founding and growth of medieval towns. Before the twelfth century almost all public administration was controlled by powerful nobles and churchmen, but the emergence of an increasingly prosperous merchant class led to the creation of merchant guilds, and regional and sometimes international trading blocks. The resulting prosperity from trade and commerce aided by regular markets and fairs led to the creation of boroughs, and burghs in northern England and Scotland. As merchant guilds grew wealthier and more influential, they demanded devolved power for local control over local matters, and powers over local administration

Left: Electricity bill issued by the Treasurer's Department at Lancaster Town Hall, 1926–27. (Author's collection)
Below: Liverpool Town Hall and square. (Postcard: author's collection)

Above left: The Grade II* Corfe Castle Old Town Hall lays claim to being England's smallest town hall building. It dates from the seventeenth century but was largely rebuilt c. 1774, and now houses the Corfe Castle Town Trust Museum. (Christine Matthews).
Above right: Chester Town Hall was built between 1865 and 1869, replacing the Old Exchange that was destroyed by fire two years earlier. Its design was based on the medieval cloth hall of Ypres, Belgium. (Colin Park)

were granted, usually by royal charter. In some places citizens were even granted the right to choose their own sheriffs and judiciary. Devolved power and economic growth created the need for new urban administrative buildings connected with trading, town governance and justice, the very essence of what became town hall functions.

The various terminology used for these buildings over the centuries can be confusing, especially as functions for same-named buildings may differ, and are not always strictly interchangeable. These include 'town hall' itself, and also town house, market house, tolsey, tollbooth, guildhall, yeldehall or yieldhall, moot or mote hall, boot or booth hall, market hall, court hall or chequer house. These 'town hall' buildings could also refer to buildings with singular functions, and so a market hall could denote a roofed market area, or it could refer to an open-sided market structure with one or more storeys housing administrative offices. A town house may be a dwelling owned by the town or a private dwelling in a town, while tolsey, toll booth or boothhall might be the term used for a small building used for toll

Above: Macclesfield's Greek Revival town hall of 1823–24 was extended in 1870 and is Grade II* listed. (Postcard: author's collection)

Below: The characterful timber-framed, Grade I listed Thaxted Guildhall, Essex, was built between 1390 and 1410 for the Guild of Curlers, and has been altered and restored several times, notably in the early eighteenth century, c. 1910 and in 1978. (Postcard: author's collection)

collection. Historian Robert Tittler identified regional naming trends, with yeldehalls usually occurring in southern England, and tolsey being an old name for a guildhall in England, notably in Oxfordshire, Gloucestershire and Wiltshire. Tollbooth is common throughout Scotland, but also in northern England, such as at Durham, Howden, Morpeth, Ripon and Whitby. It is also common in parts of East Anglia, such as Beccles and east Dereham. Boothall, or booth hall, often appears in the West Midlands and West Country, including Evesham and Gloucester.

Variation in terminology may partly be due to literal and functional descriptions of earlier buildings on the site, or structures that were expanded to provide town hall functions; this occurred at Tewkesbury, where the existing tolsey was transformed into a 'corte keeping' in 1576. On occasion, an existing name might be retained when new buildings replaced older structures, even if there was a change in function, and sometimes names may not always accurately indicate origin. Interestingly, a guildhall may not always

Above: Canongate Tolbooth, Edinburgh, was built in 1591 and served as the courthouse, gaol and council meeting place for the burgh of Canongate. (Postcard: author's collection)

Right: Tewkesbury's Grade II* listed town hall and covered marketplace was built in 1788 and was enlarged c. 1840 with a police station, cells and fire station. It was further altered in 1891. (Steve Brewer)

derive from the hall of a religious or economic guild; Evesham's gild hall in Worcestershire was not associated with any guild, and Beverley's hall in Yorkshire was originally known as the 'Hans-house' because of links with Hull's hanse merchants, until 'guildhall' was adopted after *c.* 1580. In both cases the 'guildhall' referred to the town hall. In Scotland, market jurisdiction usually came under control of the burgh and piepowder courts, which met in a tollbooth or tolsey.

A decline in the presence and influence of guilds in society followed the suppression of thousands of English guilds by the Crown in the 1530s and 1540s, and the disbanding of religious guilds. This had serious implications for the continued use of guildhall buildings. Although long-standing trade connections meant that some guildhalls retained their original use well into the nineteenth century, as at London, York and King's Lynn, others fell into disuse or were used as municipal buildings, as at Leicester, where the guildhall was used as the town hall until the mid-nineteenth century. Others were demolished and replaced with new buildings altogether, as happened at Reading, whose guildhall was demolished *c.* 1785–56 and replaced with what became known as the Small Town Hall or Victoria Hall. From the sixteenth century the growing independence of successful boroughs away from both the Church and Crown meant that markets were increasingly run by corporations that had often developed from merchant guilds.

Newent Market Hall, Gloucestershire, dates from the 1660s and was probably originally a butter market. Unlike many of its contemporaries, it is still used for market purposes today. Of special note are the heavy timber posts and semi-octagonal extension added in 1864. (Philip Halling)

Introduction

Town halls have no strict stylistic chronology, although designs often followed broader architectural trends. The medieval market hall is widely attributed as the stylistic predecessor, a building with an open arcaded ground floor, often three arches wide and three arches deep to accommodate a market, and a single first-floor room for guild and town council meetings and legal proceedings. This model originated in thirteenth-century Italy, where a centrally located combined market and town hall often situated at the head of a large and dominant square typically developed as an open, arcaded ground floor for market vendors with single council chambers and law court on the first floor. Como's Broletto of 1215, a collonaded market structure with a single first-floor room used as council chamber and law court served as the European model for centuries, although there are no British examples on the same scale until London's Guildhall of 1411–40. More usually these market house buildings were more modest, an arcaded market with administrative quarters above, variously named the aforementioned guildhall, town hall, moot hall or tolsey.

The Broletto in Como, Italy, dates to 1215 and served as the town hall of the municipality of Como. Its location adjacent to the marketplace and design with ground-floor shops and upper floors for administrative purposes were common to the location and designs of European town halls for several centuries. (Creative Commons)

Town Halls

All of the variously named town hall buildings contributed administrative, civic, judicial and market elements to town hall development down through the centuries, all remaining significant within local urban development. Alongside these, the distinct social function of the town hall can be traced from multipurpose public halls and from assembly rooms, the latter emerging in the eighteenth century to host gatherings and entertainments.

The market house was often also used for civic and social purposes, such as civic functions, court sessions and public meetings, and sometimes as a school or gaol, especially in smaller towns, where many new dual-purpose market and town hall buildings continued to be built into the seventeenth and eighteenth centuries, often surviving well into the nineteenth century. These dual-purpose buildings were often gifted by local dignitaries, as at Alcester, where the lord of the manor, Sir Fulke Greville, gave £300 for a market hall with an administrative hall above and basement gaol, which was completed in 1641. At Dursley, a new market and town hall building of 1738 replaced the old butter cross and decrepit market arcade, and had an administrative room above accessed via an external stair, and Monmouth's new hall of 1724 housed Monmouthshire's assize courts and quarter sessions as well as being used as a marketplace.

In Scotland the medieval tolbooth or townhouse continued to provide a meeting room, courthouse and sometimes a gaol, but was distinctly separate from the marketplace. Tolbooths generally retained and housed the same administrative functions into the nineteenth century and were replaced and rebuilt as required. Oldest surviving examples include those at Musselburgh (1590) and Canongate in Edinburgh (1591), which also served as the council house, courtroom and gaol.

The c. 1724 Grade I listed hall at Monmouth was designed by Philip Fisher of Bristol and accommodated the assize courts and quarter sessions for Monmouthshire as well as the market. Stylistically, it resembles halls that became more commonplace later in the century and into the next. (Gordon Hatton)

Musselburgh's tollbooth of 1590 was designed in the Scottish medieval style and constructed in ashlar stone. (Graham Hogg)

Did You Know?

Clocks and bells began to appear on town hall buildings in the sixteenth century, including a three-faced clock installed in 1591 at Shrewsbury Guildhall – one facing the interior, one facing the High Street market, and one towards the corn market.

The need for dedicated buildings serving town hall-type functions became more pressing as towns developed, with an associated need for increased local governance. There was an upsurge in the number constructed following the Reformation, indicating a development in the needs and priorities of those who governed these towns, as well as serving as symbols of local pride and rivalry. One of the earliest buildings constructed specifically for town council meetings was Fordwich Town Hall of 1544, which also served as a courtroom. However, it was not until the eighteenth century that such buildings became more commonplace within the urban landscape, constructed in response to changing and growing urban society. And it was only in the following century that the town hall was fully realised as a distinctive building type, with fully fledged municipal town halls being built in towns and cities, replacing earlier hybrid buildings and representing a golden age of urban civic pride.

Nineteenth-century town hall buildings were initially characterised by relatively simple neoclassical designs, followed by more intricate Gothic styles as the century progressed. New and more complex municipal buildings were better suited to the needs of rapidly developing towns and cities, and allowed displays of extravagance and flamboyance to represent civic greatness. This was also seen in the baroque town halls that appeared at the end of the nineteenth and early twentieth centuries. Such displays of opulence gave way to more egalitarian modernist buildings in the twentieth century, especially with the rise of civic centres as the character of local government changed, and many older civic buildings became unfit for purpose. Into the twenty-first century, new town halls are often reimagined as bold architectural statements.

The exterior and interior of Fordwich Town Hall. It was built in 1544 as a council meeting place, and also served as the town lockup. (Postcards: author's collection)

1
Eighteenth Century

Town halls were built in response to changing social, political and economic needs, and from the mid-eighteenth century the catalyst in many places was large-scale urban redevelopment, especially in towns experiencing new prosperity and wealth as a result of industrialisation. A new phase of municipal building followed a flurry of private Acts of Parliament creating various local improvement commissions to carry out specified works relating to paving, streets and general town improvements. Growing towns were provided with new developments of streets and houses, often with a centrepiece market and town hall at the head of a central public square. This was notably the case at South Shields, historically in Durham, and Stoke-on-Trent in Staffordshire, where new town hall buildings were erected in 1754 and c. 1794 respectively. As many towns were transformed into cities, especially in the Midlands and the north of England, a new town hall was essential to mark pride and status. Image was everything, and the construction of architecturally elaborate and imposing municipal buildings not only reflected civic pride, but bolstered the reputations of towns keen to prove their place and make their mark within this age of newness and change. Statement buildings reflected wealth and importance, urban organisation and identity. Larger, wealthier towns and cities often attracted eminent architects well-acquainted in the fashionable architecture of the time. Architect William Baker of Audlem designed

The eighteenth-century town hall at South Shields was set in a prime location in the marketplace. (Postcard: author's collection)

many public buildings in Shropshire and adjacent counties, including the town halls at Montgomery and Bishop's Castle, and John Wood of Bath famously designed Liverpool's town hall of 1749–54. Elsewhere local architects were employed, although their buildings were no less grand, as at Berwick-on-Tweed, which was the hub of municipal life, with a public hall-cum-courtroom and a second-floor gaol.

Montgomery Town Hall of 1748 is an exceptional example of a large, mid-eighteenth-century town and market hall, located at a central point between main streets. A ground-floor open market area had a room above for public business, including quarter sessions and Corporation meetings. (Berkelaar)

Berwick-upon-Tweed's 1754 town hall was designed by local carpenter Joseph Dods, although the plans apparently resembled those provided by Samuel and John Worrell of London. (Andrew Bowden)

Eighteenth Century

> ## Did You Know?
> Alderman Charles Poulton, designer of Reading's 1785–86 town hall was a cabinetmaker by trade.

Many of these mid- to late eighteenth-century civic buildings were aesthetically similar to grand Regency houses, externally at least. James Wyatt's neoclassical Palladian assembly room at Ripon (1798) was an impressive undertaking, but John Carr's Newark town hall was altogether more magnificent, and has been termed the country's 'finest Palladian town hall'. Designed in 1773–74 it incorporated an imposing council chamber, mayor's parlour and assembly room – a very typical interior layout, even for smaller town halls. This style continued into the nineteenth century as town halls resembling miniature mansions were built at prominent locations, many fronting market squares. Little Bolton's town hall of 1826 was relatively modest in scale, but was sited on a prominent corner with two front façades, and Middlesbrough's Italianate town hall of 1846, built at the head of the marketplace, is a very late example.

Interior decor was often elaborate and lavish, especially in larger towns and cities. Rooms and suites would be fitted with the finest furniture, and impressive staircases within grand entrances, all the better to impress. Detailed, decorative features such as friezes, cornices and marble fireplaces displayed skilled craftsmanship. Most importantly, the town arms would invariably be displayed in a prominent position at the entrance, as well as at various significant places within the building, ensuring that there could be no doubt that these were municipal buildings.

Funding of these new civic buildings could be costly, and in some places they were often privately financed by town commissioners, usually via public subscription, as was the case with the first Manchester Town Hall of *c.* 1819–45. Interestingly, markets or public rooms

Newark's magnificent 1776 town hall takes pride of place in the town centre. Designed by John Carr of York and constructed using pale Mansfield stone, it is regarded as one of the finest town halls of its era. (Postcard: author's collection)

Town Halls

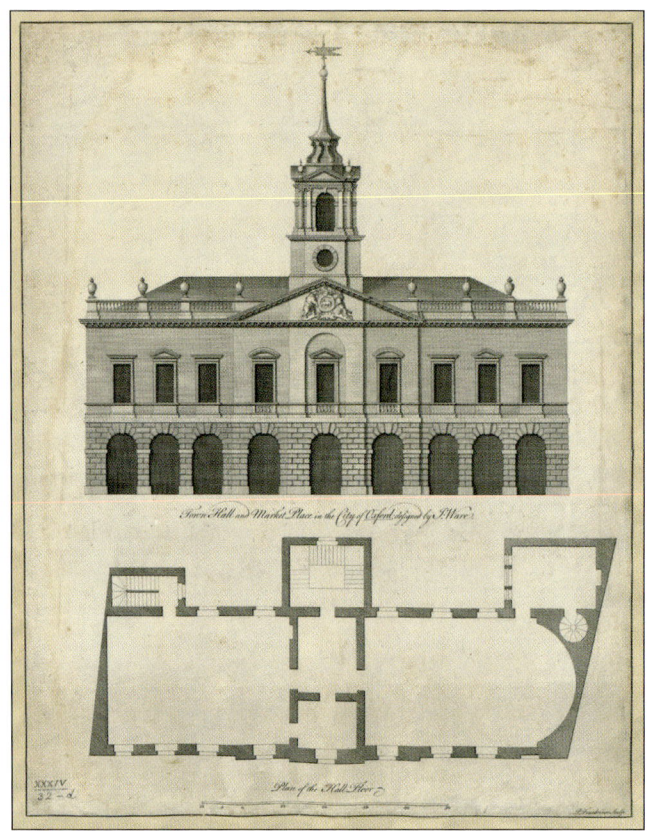

Left: Oxford Town Hall of 1752 replaced an earlier guildhall of 1292, but its simple plan and size had become inadequate by the later nineteenth century, and it was itself demolished to make way for a modern town hall in 1893. (British Library Maps, K. Top., 34.32.d.)

Below: Little Bolton Town Hall: a mansion in miniature, with a porch and paired Tuscan columns, and side door set in a rusticated surround. Without the borough arms adorning the entrance its function would probably be unclear. (Creative Commons)

Worcester's guildhall of 1721–23 has many fabulous elaborately decorated elements, including those in the assembly hall. (Rex Harris)

that had been established by public companies often developed as the town hall when town commissioners were absorbed into the workings of the new corporations. Public companies were sometimes bought out, as happened at Salford and Kidderminster. As the nineteenth century progressed, many town halls in larger towns and cities were financed by town corporations, although in smaller towns privately financed town halls were just as common, indicating a very real want and need for these buildings. Bourne Town Hall of 1821 was built by public subscription on land donated to the town by the Marquess of Exeter. At St Andrews, donations from Fife's citizens and nobility were supplemented by fundraising, enabling a much-needed new town hall to be built, as befitted the town's status; the existing building had become unviable by the 1850s, too small to accommodate the large numbers of people attending various events, and deemed detrimental to the town's image as a place of education and historical interest because of its shapeless and ugly appearance.

A profusion of limited town hall companies were established in the mid- to late nineteenth century, enabling the purchase of shares by a town's citizens to fund new town hall buildings. Importantly, shareholders could attend town hall meetings, often annually, to discuss, debate and decide matters relating to the town hall building itself. These could be as varied as approving event applications and determining the form of extensions and extent of building works.

Despite this citizen ownership some new town halls were occasionally gifted by local worthies, as in earlier periods. Meltham's new town hall of 1898 was funded and donated by local manufacturer and philanthropist Edward Brook, and Maesteg's town hall of 1881

No. 77 CERTIFICATE OF SHARE. £5.

BILLERICAY
TOWN HALL COMPANY,
LIMITED.

INCORPORATED PURSUANT TO ACT OF PARLIAMENT.

CAPITAL, £1000 IN 200 SHARES of £5 each.

This is to certify that James Jefferies of Great Burstead in the County of Essex Farmer is the Proprietor of the Share Number 77 of the BILLERICAY TOWN HALL COMPANY, LIMITED, subject to the Regulations of the said Company, and that up to this day there has been paid up in respect of such Share the sum of One Pound.—

Given under the Common Seal of the said Company, the 21st day of January in the year 1863.

SECRETARY. DIRECTORS.

Billericay Town Hall Company share certificate. (Essex Record Office, 18A/57/KS)

Side view of Mansfield's 1835–36 civic building, from Market Street. Funded by a town hall company, it was essentially an early 'complete' town hall with a formal design. A grand entrance led into a formal front block containing all main rooms, and a large assembly hall occupied the whole first floor. A lock-up, offices and shambles were located to the rear. (Dave Bevis)

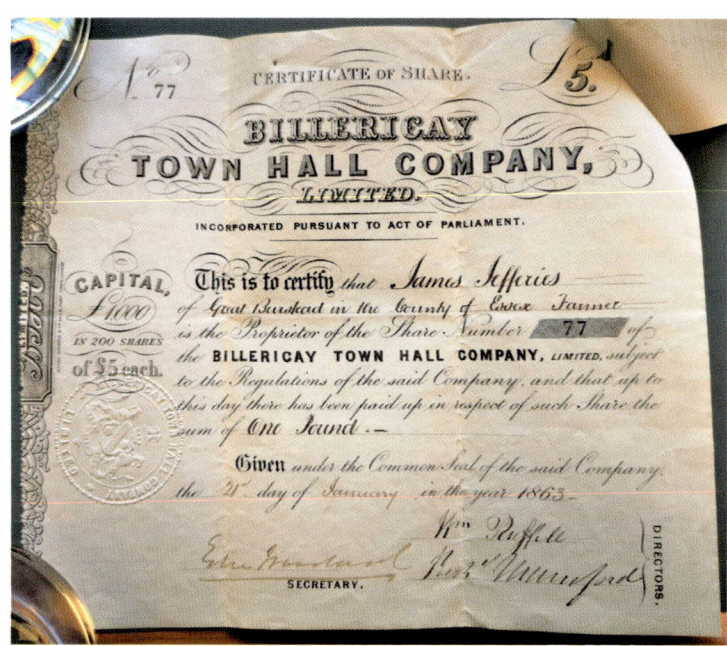

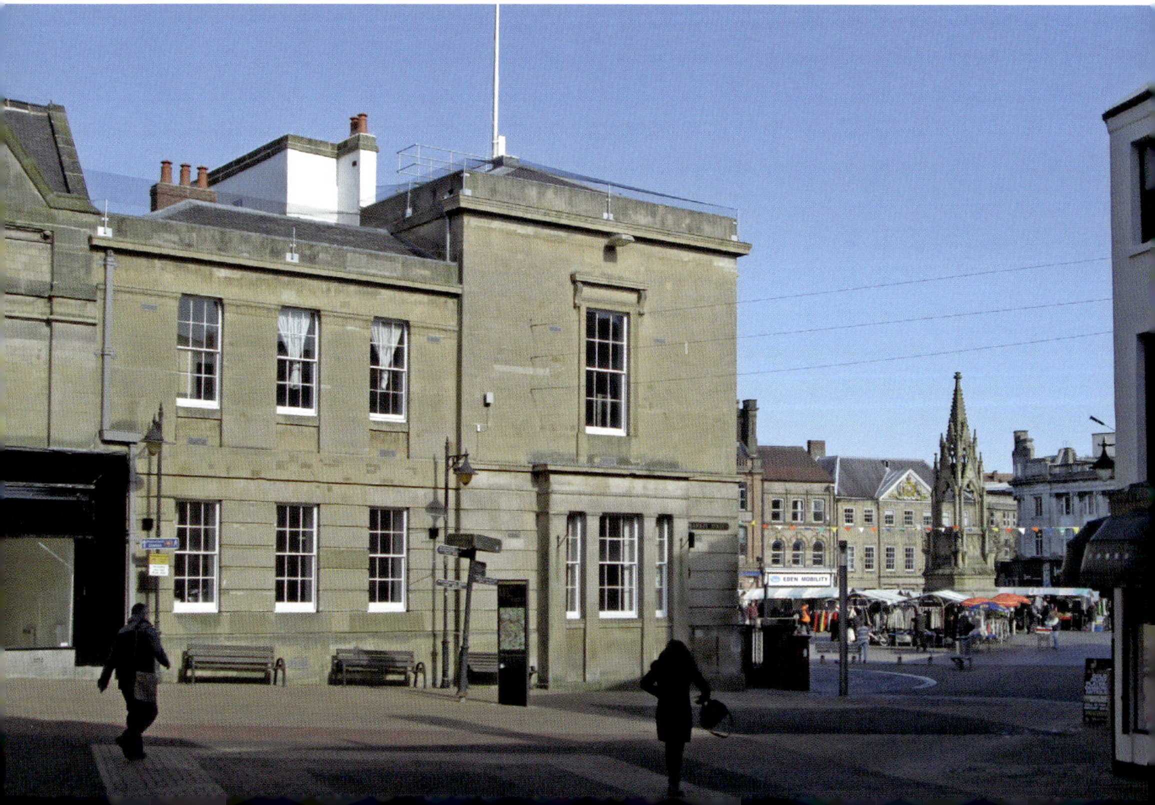

was funded in part by local landowner, industrialist and MP Christopher Talbot, although it was also part-funded by a levy of a day's wages from the valley miners. Sometimes existing buildings were donated rather than the provision of funding for a brand-new town hall, as happened at Burton-on-Trent in 1891 when Lord Burton gifted St Paul's Institute and Liberal Club buildings to convert for town hall use.

Elsewhere, existing public buildings were remodelled, especially in smaller towns such as Devizes, where an earlier seventeenth-century building was incorporated into the new town hall of 1806–08, and Montgomery, where in 1828 the upper storey of the existing town hall was raised and a flat-roofed extension to the rear of the building was added. In 1870s Walthamstow, where swift urbanisation was taking hold, the need for a new town hall to house council affairs and to greet and entertain visiting dignitaries was realised through incorporating the existing public hall within a new building. Unfortunately, many of the dual-purpose town and market halls that had served their towns so well over the years were generally unsuitable for conversion: they were simply too small, and adjacent space rarely allowed reconfiguration and extension. Some were demolished in this period, as at Burton-on-Trent, whose obsolete town hall at the head of the marketplace was demolished in 1883, although, happily, many more have survived, especially in market towns where they contribute to the historic character of their surroundings.

Despite reuse and adaptation of existing buildings in some places, sweeping changes in nineteenth-century local government and urban life ensured a dominant presence for new town halls that were built in cities and larger towns throughout the country. These coincided with bold changes in architectural fashions, and so the town hall proper emerged as a significant presence within the urban landscape and became one of the most significant building types of the nineteenth century, as a swathe of new monumental buildings were dramatically realised in meticulously planned designs.

The elegant, two-storey, Grade II* Devizes Town Hall in Wiltshire of 1806–08 incorporated parts of the preceding earlier seventeenth-century building. (Michael Day)

Left: Walthamstow Old Town Hall: The sloping roofline of the earlier public hall it incorporated is visible just beneath the bulb of the lamppost on the right. (Jay Garrett)
Below: Rather than embracing new, modern design, the red-brick town hall built at Marlborough in 1901–02 was somewhat of a seventeenth-century throwback, with its steeply pitched roof, dormers and wide eaves. It was the last of a succession of town halls built on the same site dating back to *c.* 1630. (Author's collection)

2
Nineteenth Century

The changes that enabled this town hall revolution in the mid- to later nineteenth century were far-reaching. Local corporations had largely become unrepresentative and self-interested, comprised, as they mostly were, of privileged Tory and Anglican freemen. The Municipal Reform Act of 1835 went some way to change this, and established 178 municipal corporations, each governed by an elected council, creating the basis for municipal unity and reorganisation. A spate of new municipal town halls did not immediately follow, however, as provision of many services initially remained under the control of town commissioner boards, and although the Act allowed transference of these powers to new corporations, some boroughs remained under commissioner control into the 1880s. Nevertheless, the stage was set.

Growing urbanisation, too, was central to the emergence of the fully formed town hall. Most of the country's population was decidedly rural at the start of the nineteenth century, but by 1851 over 50 per cent of the population were town dwellers. This expediential growth resulted in a series of Acts and an array of new regulations relating to public health and housing issues, and so created a need for dedicated civic premises for an ever-increasing number of services. The incorporation of new towns invariably preceded construction of new town halls, especially from the later 1850s, as at Morley, Leigh and Rochdale.

Later in the century Local Government Acts of 1888 and 1894 introduced a comprehensive pattern of district, parish and county councils, partly to reduce overlapping authorities and to simplify local administration. The 1888 Act also created sixty-one county boroughs from large or historically significant urban areas that fell beyond county council administration.

Although there was never a singular town hall style or type, many new purpose-built town halls of the nineteenth century were fronted by a public square or open space, as were their predecessors, but many were now also provided with fine landscaped gardens, also open to the public. The building itself invariably incorporated a suite of civic areas, with council chamber, meeting and/or banqueting room, first-floor mayoral accommodation above street level and suites of administrative offices. By the end of the nineteenth century, many new town halls were often surmounted by a tower.

The council chamber and mayor's suite for municipal functions were naturally key components of new town halls of this period, but spaces for public events were also significant, often with large assembly rooms to host civic occasions as well as public concerts. Liverpool's neoclassical complex of St George's Hall, begun in 1841, perhaps best represents the pinnacle of a successful combination of the concert hall and municipal functions. But it was Birmingham that lays claim to be the first monumental purpose-built town hall, an excellent example of nineteenth century classical revival architecture, styled on Rome's Temple of Castor and Pollux. Other neoclassical designed town halls followed, including that at Burslem of 1854, notable for its life-sized gilded copper angel of Victory, and Paisley of 1882.

Classical designs were initially successful in accommodating the various required civic elements, when a single committee room in the basement was sufficient. But town hall

Town Hall Square, Bexhill. (Postcard: author's collection)

Croydon's 1898 town hall and its adjacent gardens. (Postcard: author's collection)

THE TOWN HALL, BIRMINGHAM, DURING THE FESTIVAL.

THE QUEEN'S ARRIVAL AT THE TOWN HALL, BIRMINGHAM.

Spot the difference. Birmingham's Grade I listed town hall of 1834 originally had thirteen columns along each side, but was later extended to accommodate an organ, with the addition of two extra columns. The first image depicts an undated festival procession, probably the Birmingham Musical Festival, and the second shows the arrival of Queen Victoria in 1858. (Birmingham Museums image collections, 1996V146.28 and 1970V1134)

Paisley Town Hall of 1882 was built primarily as a public hall to the south of other municipal buildings. It was funded by money bequeathed for the purpose by George Aitken Clark, of a renowned mill-owning family. (Postcard: author's collection)

requirements changed due to increasingly complex bureaucracy, and as more specialist departments requiring more staff were created, classical designs posed many planning and construction problems involving fitting an increasing number of disparate offices, halls and committee rooms into a single block.

Gothic designs became predominant in new town hall design, as they provided more flexibility in both design and cost, more easily allowing irregular layout and easier extension. Manchester and Leeds are especially notable for their magnificently imposing and complex town halls. Manchester had outgrown its earlier neoclassical town hall and in 1863–64 a much grander affair was planned on an irregular triangular site, within which a large hall, suite of reception rooms, mayoral quarters, corporation offices and council chamber needed to be sited. A competition attracting 137 entries was won by one Alfred Waterhouse, who successfully combined the ceremonial and municipal requirements executed with a medieval Gothic design that incorporated modern elements, notably a warm air heating system. Leeds Town Hall (1853–58) was designed by renowned Gothic architect Cuthbert Brodrick, and included law courts, a council chamber, offices, public hall and a suite of ceremonial rooms, topped with an impressive colonnaded tower. This successful town hall design was emulated elsewhere, notably at Morley, Portsmouth and Bolton.

The fully developed town hall was extremely complex as municipal bureaucracy reached its zenith, with warrens of segregated departments, multiple entrances and staircases. By the later nineteenth century new town halls were vast complexes of council chambers, committee rooms, meeting and civic reception rooms, banquet halls and offices. Office accommodation

Bolton's neoclassical town hall of 1866–73 was rectangular in plan with a tall, baroque clocktower. (Postcard: author's collection)

in suites rather than singular offices could house an army of various departmental clerks working within an increasing variety of municipal departments. Integral substantial and well-appointed rooms as part of both the entertainment suite and council proceedings were essential to civic display; it was crucial that the mayor was able to receive and impress formal visitors in surroundings that created an atmosphere of dignity and wealth that reflected the

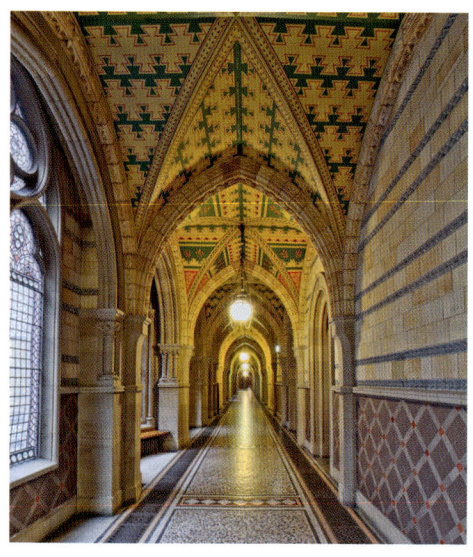

Left: Manchester Town Hall's interior. Construction of the building took nine years at a cost of £521,537 for the building itself, and *c.* £859,000 for land, furnishings and fees. (Michael Heskwith)
Below: Ground-floor plan, Edinburgh Town Hall, 1887. (*The Builder*, Vol. 52, 1887)

Edinburgh Municipal Buildings: Design by Messrs. Hay & Henderson.—Plan at High-street Level.

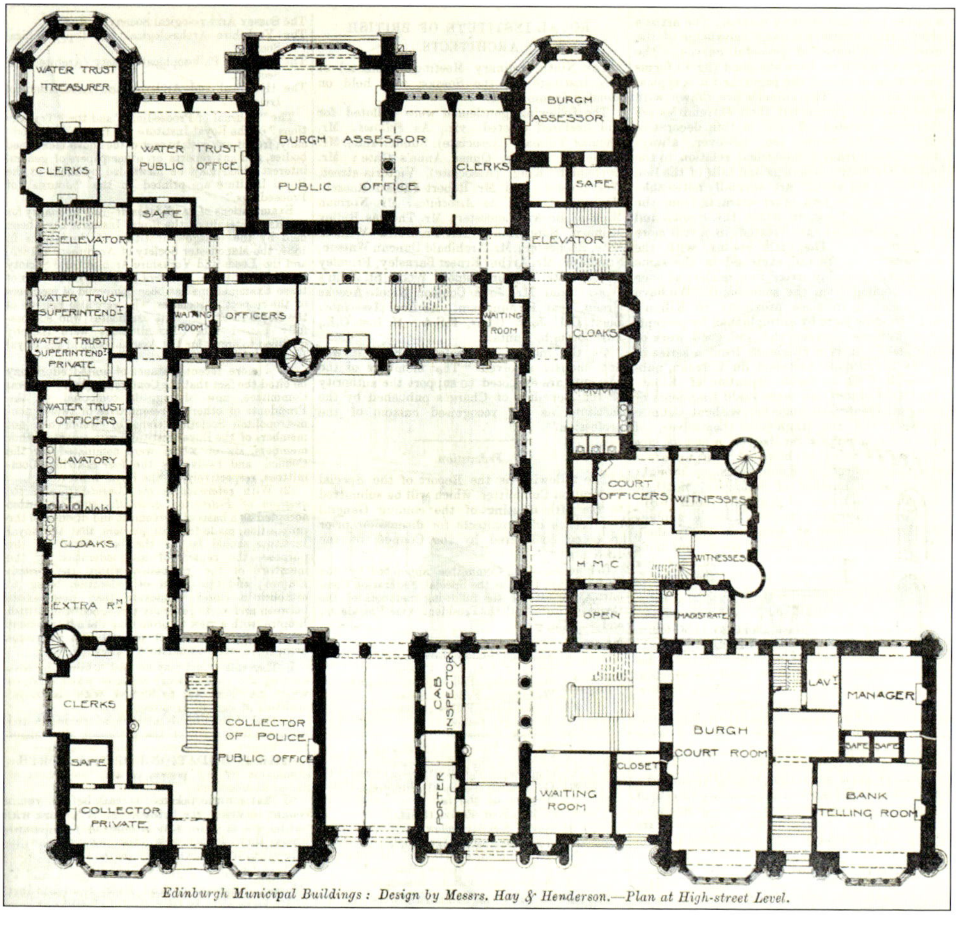

greatness of the town or city. Accordingly, interior decor had to be impressive and lavish and extravagant features were as integral to new town hall design as the building's layout.

As hall space became larger with galleries and permanent seating, they were more unsuited to certain functions such as banquets, and so in many places a separate banqueting hall was provided, often adjacent to or ensuite with the mayoral apartments. Both Morley's town hall of 1892–95 and Hove's of 1880–81 had a great hall and smaller banqueting hall, and at Manchester a complete 'mansion house' was inserted between the banqueting hall and offices. Where entertainment venues already existed, such as Bradford's St George's Hall, with a 4000-person capacity, there was no need for a new town hall to include a large hall and so the design could focus on municipal and business facilities.

As new public services emerged in response to the improvement of urban life, many new complexes also incorporated art galleries and reading rooms, the latter often developing into the town or city library. Some town halls even included technical or design schools, although this only generally occurred at smaller towns or subdistricts of larger towns. Other essential services such as baths and wash houses were less easy to house within town hall complexes, especially as they needed to be geographically closer to those who needed them and were therefore only found within town halls serving smaller townships, such as Yardley's town hall of 1898, then in the county of Worcestershire. The size of these new municipal complexes depended upon the size of the urban area they were built to serve and could be extremely vast.

It was not uncommon for other municipal services to be incorporated into town hall complexes such as fire and police stations, and centrally located complexes comprising these and a public hall and municipal offices began to appear. These complexes were sometimes the result of piecemeal development, although later examples were often typically adjacent and built in the same design, as at Lancaster, where a baroque town

Lancaster's baroque town hall and adjacent fire station. (*Architecture*, 1906)

Police cells in the basement at Grimsby Town Hall are now used by North East Lincolnshire Archives. (Author's collection)

hall of 1906–09 was flanked by a smaller stylistically similar fire station. New design elements had to be incorporated, such as exercise yards and police parade space, and a police station with cells was essential if the town hall contained court space. Although classical designs had easily accommodated hidden cells in the podium, ventilation had proved to be an issue, and new designs therefore needed to include cells located in an above-ground location. Other elements that needed to be incorporated in these complexes included living accommodation for a live-in caretaker, as well as more substantial housing for police and fire superintendents.

Although other architectural styles also appeared in this period, such as Leicester's Queen Anne town hall of 1874–76, and Sheffield's town hall of 1891–97, designed to complement the exterior of the adjacent St Paul's Church of 1720, baroque designs that emerged in the later nineteenth and remained commonplace until c. 1914 were better suited to the segregation of different departments, with formal official departments easily accommodated within the frontages. The style allowed for considerable extravagance, as at Plumstead's municipal buildings of 1899, Cardiff's of 1900–04 and Jarrow's town hall, which was completed c. 1902.

Some designs were less successful than others, however, and as the town hall continued to evolve some plans proved problematic. Middlesbrough's 1880s complex was rather awkward, with ten entrances and at least thirteen staircases, and a warren of segregated departments, but no internal circulation to allow ease of movement between them. Some new buildings proved unsuitable alarmingly quickly, but increasing pressures to extend were potentially expensive and restricted by available space. Bolton's accommodation had reached critical mass by the 1890s, yet new building did not take place until the 1930s, and as a result departments were scattered throughout the town in different offices. Others fared better, including Leeds Town Hall, with several subsequent expansion and improvement phases beginning relatively soon after completion, as it contained relatively few internal departments and offices. Occasionally, architects planned for future expansion, as appears to have happened at Sheffield, extended shortly after the town hall of 1891–97 was completed, and at Barrow-in-Furness, whose design at competition stage was required to have several phases. However, most additions

Above: Jarrow's distinctive terracotta and red brick Baroque town hall of 1902 was designed by South Shields architect Fred Rennoldson. The three-sided clock was a later 1950s addition. (Phil Payne)
Below: Middlesbrough Town Hall was designed by G. D. Hoskins and completed in 1883–89. (Tom Bastin)

Sheffield's magnificent town hall tower. (Chris Morgan)

were unplanned, evidenced by the many examples where extensions were executed in different architectural styles. Fortunately, some were complementary rather than jarring, as with Manchester's town hall extension and library of 1925.

Interestingly, as office space grew larger in relation to showier display elements the town hall was largely indistinguishable from other large building types, which may explain why towers became a recurrent and dominant feature on new town halls by the end of the nineteenth century, marking the town hall out in the landscape. Particularly impressive is the Victoria Tower at Colchester Town Hall, standing 162 feet tall, with its clock and peal of five bells. The tower is crowned with a bronze statue of Empress Helena, one of the town's historical worthies, and is adorned with four bronze ravens symbolising the port of Colchester, and allegorical stone figures representing Engineering, Fishery, Agriculture and Military Defence. Sheffield's town hall of 1897 has an imposing 210-foot clock tower at the north corner, set back slightly from the main façade. Very fittingly, the tower is topped with a 2.13-metre statue of Vulcan, Roman god of fire and metalworking, and has four clock dials, each measuring 2.5 metres in diameter.

Did You Know?

The design of Sheffield Town Hall's clock tower originally included a set of bells, but they were never installed. In 2002 an electronic bell sound system was inserted into the tower to provide an hourly strike and Palace of Westminster-style quarter chimes.

3
Twentieth Century

The reasons behind the construction of so many town halls were often practical, with the purpose-built new replacing the inadequate old, but the need for new town halls also arose following boundary changes, especially where areas were absorbed and new boroughs established. The 1888 and 1894 Acts permitted the expansion of county boroughs, and towns with a population of over 50,000 could apply for county borough status. As a result, twenty-three new county boroughs were created by 1922, which often incorporated further territory on an ad hoc basis, usually in response to urban growth. Expansion of other urban jurisdictions was also significant, as at Portobello, where a new town hall of 1912 was the result of provisions in the Edinburgh Extension Act for the city to build and maintain a new town hall there. However, alongside the need for new town halls, the absorption and merging of parishes or boundary changes meant that some town halls became defunct, as happened at Limehouse. Following the absorption of the civil parish of Limehouse into the metropolitan borough of Stepney in 1900, the town hall was no longer a seat of local government and was subsequently converted to use as offices.

In London where vestry halls had performed town hall functions in most London parishes until the 1880s, the creation of new metropolitan boroughs meant that new town halls were

Portobello's new town hall opened in 1914. Its first public event was a concert in aid of displaced Belgian refugees. (Postcard: author's collection)

required in most areas. Despite serving larger urban populations these new halls were often small as site values were high, and so they were not usually overly grandiose or ornamental, although some outer borough town halls were more architecturally flamboyant as at Deptford. Classical or baroque designs were usually favoured over Gothic, although internal arrangements were generally the same for both styles, with a large hall, committee rooms and offices. Many were constructed of red brick and had a Westmorland slate roof, marking them out as municipal buildings, while others had Portland stone as the predominant building material, as at St Pancras (1892) or Bethnal Green (1909–10).

New early twentieth-century town halls varied little in form and function from their predecessors of previous decades, although the number of new town halls being built was considerably less. However, the advent of the First World War in 1914 brought about an abrupt change of use for a handful of town halls, albeit temporarily, including some newly completed or in the throes of completion. These buildings were repurposed as auxiliary hospitals for the duration of the war, sometimes with immediate effect, to alleviate the overwhelming pressure on existing domestic and military hospitals from an estimated 1.6 million British soldier casualties requiring treatment and rehabilitation. Waltham Abbey Town Hall was transformed into an auxiliary military hospital within weeks of receiving orders on 24 November 1914, receiving its first patients on 5 December that same year, and Torquay's brand-new town hall, completed in 1913, was transformed in October 1914 into a fifty-bed Red Cross Town Hall Hospital. The new town hall at Wallasey, Merseyside, was earmarked for use as a war hospital while still under construction. For most town halls, however, it was pretty much business as usual, although many were venues for wartime-related domestic events, especially fundraising for various causes.

The Grade II listed 'modified baroque' Lambeth Town Hall of 1905–08 was constructed in red brick with Portland stone dressings. (Postcard: author's collection)

Wallasey Town Hall was transformed into a military hospital for the duration of the First World War. Over 3,500 casualties were admitted there – mostly soldiers from Wallasey, Wirral and the wider local area. (Wirral Library Services, BPL1772C)

Did You Know?

Two notable literary figures worked at the Torquay Town Hall Auxiliary Hospital, where they became friends: novelist Agatha Christie, who was engaged there as a nurse from October 1914, and poet Alberta Vickridge, a member of the Voluntary Aid Detachment from 1917. Christie apparently worked in the hospital dispensary where she leaned about poisons, taking the Apothecaries Hall exam in 1917.

Post-war, town hall buildings continued their evolution as a distinct building type, demanding new approaches and new buildings in response to changing boundaries and the changing nature of local government. Many municipal buildings were constructed in this interwar period, and although singular town halls were built, town hall buildings were more often part of larger municipal complexes or civic centres.

The four main components of town hall buildings – namely municipal offices, an assembly hall, mayoral reception rooms and law courts – had been hitherto very clearly defined, with an emphasis on the very showy ceremonial element as a very separate and significant entity to that of business administrative element, which was largely hidden from the public gaze. In this period the emphasis shifted, and municipal offices became the largest component

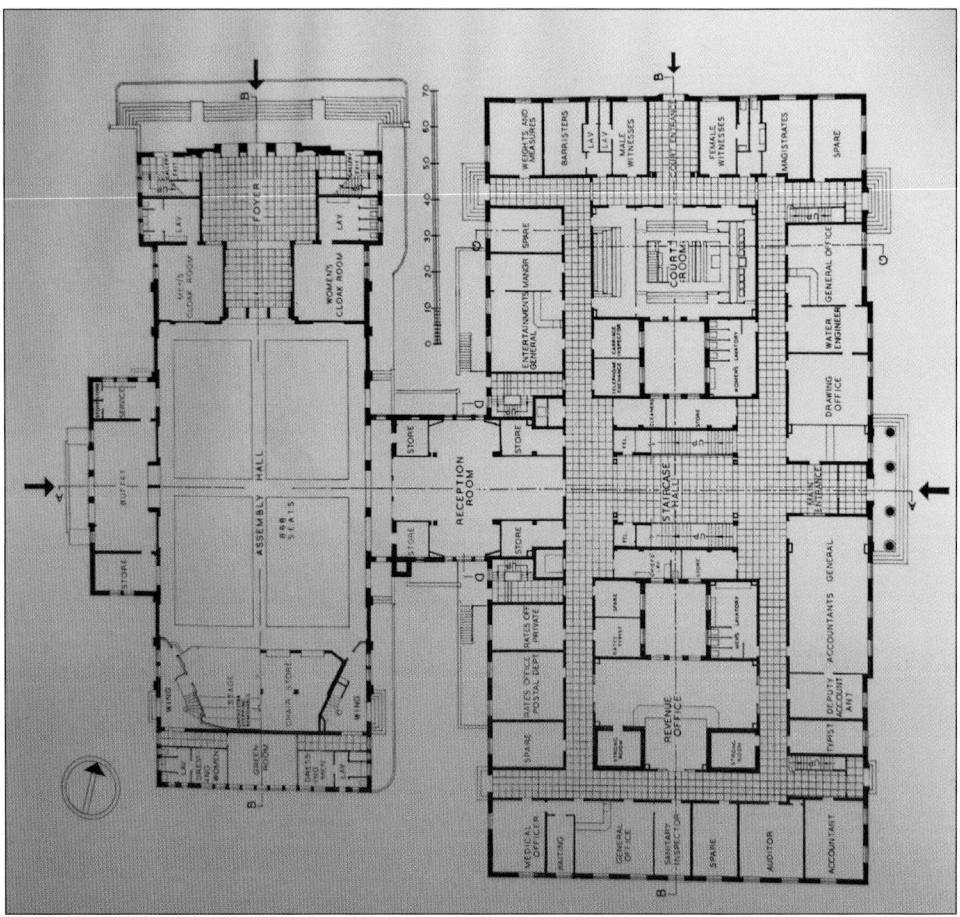

Ground-floor plan of Worthing Town Hall. Designed by Charles Cowles-Voysey in a neo-Georgian style, it replaced the earlier 1835 town hall. The new municipal complex included offices, a council chamber and an assembly hall to the rear. (A. Calverley-Cotton)

within an arrangement of increasingly interwoven municipal and ceremonial rooms. Whereas in earlier town hall buildings, ceremonial rooms, mayoral suites and assembly rooms had been largely the preserve of the mayor and invited guests to the exclusion of the general public, ceremonial elements were now often reduced to a single room and the mayoral rooms were essentially sidelined. These changes were partly due to lack of money and space, and partly because after the First World War entertaining and hospitality never quite resumed on such a lavish scale.

The hallmark of these new municipal complexes was efficient planning, taking into account this shift in requirements. The mayoral role remained largely ceremonial, and so mayoral rooms did not need to be connected with the council chamber, committee rooms or municipal offices. Committee rooms did not need to be close to the council chamber, although they were required to adjoin the municipal offices to allow easy access to reference material during meetings. Where committee rooms also doubled as reception rooms, at least

The Grade II* listed Braintree Town Hall, pictured here in 1955, opened in 1928 and is an early example of a building constructed using reinforced concrete, which was used in the foundations, floor and roof. (Postcard: author's collection)

two or three were necessary to avoid interruptions by mayoral receptions – most committee meetings and council meeting were held at night as councillors were often unable to attend in daytimes. Lastly, the council chamber did not need to be near to the committee rooms or any departments, and could be located in the main body of rooms with circulation.

The assembly hall of previous eras was usually a large room attached to the ceremonial suite, banqueting room or ballroom, exclusively for local authority use. By contrast, the interwar assembly hall was a versatile entertainment venue located away from the ceremonial rooms, and, importantly, could be hired by the public for dances, meetings, lectures and concerts as a separate entity.

Interior plans were based upon a model that rarely deviated. A grand entrance hall and staircase led to the first-floor council chamber (normally located towards the rear of the building with the committee rooms) and mayor's parlour, and associated rooms were arranged along the front. Office accommodation occupying one large space allowed fluidity and easy adaption to meet a variety of changes as different departments changed in size over time. Planning considerations new to this period related to better public access and amenities, including lavatories and the location of a press table.

These municipal buildings were usually the result of the competition system, which was especially successful in this period. Many renowned architects began their careers with winning entries for municipal buildings, among them Berry Webber, Percy Thomas and Charles Cowles-Voysey. Braintree's town hall of 1928 was designed by Emanuel Vincent Harris, whose other notable buildings include the Ministry of Defence building and Leeds Civic Hall. Bradshaw Gass & Hope, noted for their classically influenced buildings, designed several town halls between 1928 and 1939, including the neoclassical Trafford Town Hall, which was completed in 1933.

Did You Know?

In 1933 the derelict town hall in Newtown, Isle of Wight, was donated to the National Trust by Ferguson's Gang, a diverse group of young women who wore masks and used pseudonyms such as Sister Agatha and Bill Stickers. Frustrated by the steady destruction of the countryside and historic places, they travelled the country opposing development and construction in historic locations and regularly donated money to the National Trust in unconventional ways. The town hall was the second building to be saved by the group.

Poplar Town Hall is particularly notable for its mosaic frieze and a series of Portland stone relief sculptures by David Evans, depicting the trades that constructed the town hall – carpenter, labourer, stonemason and architect. (Jim Osley)

Many 1920s civic buildings were built to classical revival designs, although were generally more austere than their nineteenth-century predecessors. Some of those built in the 1930s fell within the art deco camp, Norwich City Hall of 1938 and Worthing's 1933 town hall being especially worthy of note, but by the 1930s modernist designs were generally more favoured. These were especially suited to municipal buildings and often had marble facings, wood veneers and specially designed furniture. This outwardly modernist style coincided with a period of local government's central role in an unprecedented public investment in social housing, health and educational facilities, although only progressive councils commissioned modernist buildings. The first truly modernist town hall is Poplar's 1938 building, described by Historic England as the first town hall built on pure modern lines, its artwork testifying 'to the aspirations of the Borough of Poplar in the interwar years' being especially significant. The mosaic frieze above the entrance and carved Portland stone panels commemorated the workers' trades that constructed the town hall and symbolised the borough's relationship with the River Thames and the youth of Poplar.

Did You Know?

In the 1930s it was reported that seven out of ten people got immediately lost upon entering any town hall. (A. Calveley Cotton, 1936)

Twentieth Century

Above: Worker bee motif on the floor of Manchester Town Hall's entrance hall. (Gareth Hacking)
Below: Walthamstow's civic complex was designed with a central town hall (completed in 1942) flanked by an assembly hall and law courts. Lack of sufficient funds meant that the original design remained incomplete and although the assembly hall was completed in 1943, the law courts were not built until the 1970s. (Dave Art Gordon)

Modernist Scandinavian design influenced several London borough civic buildings, including those at Hammersmith, Greenwich, Hornsey and Walthamstow, the latter being an especially good example as the town hall is the central and most important part of the borough's new civic complex. Influences of such design is occasionally seen outside of London, including the portico of Norwich City Hall.

In the Second World War the role of the town hall remained much the same administratively, although practical measures were implemented in some places to protect the buildings and occupants. Luton's dazzling white stone clock tower was camouflaged so that it did not become an obvious target during air raids, and at Wembley Town Hall a bombproof first-aid post was installed. In fact, this town hall was one of a handful completed in wartime, opening in 1940. Constructed of brick rather than concrete, it was later described by Nikolaus Pevsner as 'the best of the modern town halls around London, neither fanciful nor drab'.

Many town halls were the focus of war-related events, often involving special entertainments or services, and benefit or fundraising events, as at Portsmouth Town Hall where the Committee of the Portsmouth Heroes Fund held regular teas and entertainments for war-wounded, with groceries donated by local businesses. At Hawick, Roxburghshire, Sunday evening services held by St George's Church for townsfolk and serving military billeted to the town proved extremely popular, often with standing room only.

Did You Know?

Advice for design of interwar civic centres published by A. Calveley Cotton in 1936 stated that there should be a separate small sink for washing inkpots in clerk toilets.

Post-war development and recovery had a significant impact upon town halls, both new buildings and the use of the old. Many larger towns and cities were subject to large-scale redevelopment, the most ambitious schemes being the creation of several new towns following the 1946 New Towns Act and 1947 Local Government (Scotland) Act, intended to alleviate housing shortages and accommodate population overspills. These included Crawley, Stevenage and Harlow, whose new town halls of the 1950s and 1960s were a significant part of town planning. The architecture of these new towns were characterised by modern buildings built for the people, and their new town halls are often associated with public areas containing public art. Town halls of this period were essential for the shaping of a new and modern identity, and brutalist design offered a practical and modern design solution for governance in this new age. Darlington's new town hall of 1970 was a key component within the new civic centre, bringing together the various council offices, which had hitherto been dispersed throughout the town. Sited next to St Cuthbert's Church and the marketplace, it occupied the traditional central and dominant location for town halls. Hove's bold new town hall of 1970–73 replaced its Gothic predecessor that had been destroyed by fire in 1966 and offered something completely different. Its irregular plan housed a council chamber, mayoral suite, offices and committee rooms over three levels, and a great hall cantilevered over a public piazza. Notable town hall extensions of this period to accommodate additional office accommodation include Wallasey's South Annexe of 1964, Camden Town Hall's annexe of 1973–78 and Stockport's Stopford House, which opened in 1975.

Twentieth Century

Did You Know?

Stopford House, the 1975 extension to Stockport's town hall, was the police station in TV series *Life on Mars*.

The advent of new modern architectural landscapes often included the sweeping away of old; older and former town hall buildings that were not in keeping with new visions of forward thinking and modernity were demolished, as at Stevenage, where demolition of its village town hall made way for a new gyratory system, and at Bridgend and Newcastle, whose town halls were lost in 1971 and 1973. Elsewhere town redevelopment schemes worked around existing town halls and other older buildings, notably at Plymouth, and as in previous eras, the need for a new town hall was very occasionally met by converting existing buildings, although this was relatively rare.

By the 1980s and 1990s many older town halls still in use were outdated, unfit for purpose, and badly in need of renovation, as the fate of scores of municipal buildings throughout the country hung in the balance. Some were demolished, as happened at Ludlow in 1986, but elsewhere local authorities had sufficient budgets and the will to refurbish their premises or else repurpose them for other council use, as was the case for Richmond Town Hall, which was converted for use by the library service. In Reading, plans drawn up in the 1980s to demolish the town hall and replace it with a new cultural centre were dropped in favour of a refurbishment programme between 1986 and 2000, bringing its concert hall back into use and providing several new galleries for the town's museum and art gallery. Other town halls

The design of Stevenage Town Hall included public space and artwork located at the front of the building. (Postcard: author's collection)

Left: Hove Town Hall is a bold and striking building with a monumental main entrance. Its equally striking interior includes a grand entrance foyer with a staircase sweeping up to two floors, and it originally incorporated an indoor garden. (Hassocks)
Below: Stockport's brutalist Stopford House opened in 1975 as much-needed additional council office accommodation. (Gene Hunt)

Richmond Town Hall is now home to the museum, library and archives. (Author's collection)

were sold for redevelopment in the private sector, such as Rotherham Old Town Hall, which was converted to a shopping centre in the 1980s, and Poplar Town Hall, which was converted for commercial use in the 1990s and subsequently used as a business centre.

New town halls were built very occasionally in the later twentieth century and into the twenty-first, such as Cumbernauld New Town Hall, a multipurpose venue of 1996 with business and community spaces, and London's City Hall of 2002, which was built at a cost of around £43 million. Elsewhere, the need for new town hall buildings was circumvented by acquiring unused buildings in the locale, as happened with Wigan Town Hall, which was relocated to the former Wigan Mining and Technical College building of 1903. But generally, wholly new town hall schemes were rarer, as municipal buildings have been subject to large redevelopment and refurbishment schemes as part of council attempts to balance the preservation of local heritage and provision and maintenance local council services within budgetary and spending restrictions.

Cumbernauld's multipurpose town hall was built in 1996 and offers the local community and businesses a range of facilities, as well as housing the office of the Registrar of Births, Deaths and Marriages. The two-storey glazed entrance hall leads to two function suites on the ground and first floors. (Ann Giles)

4
Twenty-first Century

Town halls remain central to daily life in their continued role of providing essential public services for local residents, although the physical location of administrative offices providing these services is no longer guaranteed to be located in a landmark purpose-built municipal building. Local authorities face ongoing and recurrent difficult financial decisions as a result of reductions in central government funding, and where municipal buildings are costly to maintain options to retain these are limited. Restoration and renovation schemes are expensive and many councils have opted to downsize to smaller premises and sell off their historic town halls and other municipal buildings in money-saving exercises, especially where town hall sites occupy prime real estate land. Investment in new council buildings often goes hand in hand with the sale of the old, although local authorities occasionally opt to rent office space rather than construct new office accommodation.

Nevertheless, there have been successful large-scale regeneration schemes involving existing town hall sites, although these can be controversial within local communities especially when heritage buildings are threatened or compromised. Such redevelopment visions often have to be pragmatic and are monetised where possible with the inclusion of private sector elements, often with the leasing of office space or venue hire. Unsurprisingly, redevelopment schemes in the south-east, especially in London boroughs, are big business, and several twentieth-century town halls and civic centres have undergone twenty-first-century transformations, some including housing and cultural community hubs.

The helical walkway at London's City Hall ascends the building's ten stories, winding for an impressive 500 metres. (Colin)

Crawley's old town hall, with the adjacent new town hall under construction. (Mark Tandy)

Despite being extended several times, Crawley's 1950s town hall eventually became unfit for purpose and its demolition and replacement by a new, nine-storey town hall with a civic centre and council chamber on the same site began early in 2020. The new development incorporated a customer services space, revenue-generating commercial office space and private and affordable housing, while the creation of a new landscaped public square echoed the traditional town square. Hounslow's Civic Centre, too, had also outlived any practical use, becoming unfit for purpose, and high running costs in particular were a major concern. Downsizing to a smaller building was an essential cost-saving exercise, allowing the site to be redeveloped for much-needed housing. New town centre council premises opened in 2019 within a purpose-built office building that provided smaller and more energy-efficient accommodation for the civic suite and council chamber, which could also be hired as a community or event space. As well as adult education classrooms, Hounslow Library, along with health and police partners, were also accommodated, harking back to the multipurpose town hall complexes of earlier periods.

Did You Know?

Several municipal buildings had Cold War bunkers, control centres or stand-by centres installed in the 1960s and 1970s, including Essex County Hall, Hereford and Worcester County Hall and Darlington Town Hall.

Above: Hounslow's new town hall building, Hounslow House, opened in 2019, replacing the former Civic Centre. The new building housed all council administrative departments and the council chamber as well being a venue for other community services, including adult education classes. (Author's collection)
Below: The Royal London Hospital site was chosen as the location for the new Tower Hamlets Town Hall, although only the façade of the original eighteenth-century building was retained. (Ian S.)

Ambitious redevelopment plans for Waltham Forest's civic complex were approved in 2020. They included the transformation of the site to create a brand-new neighbourhood and cultural hub with affordable and market value housing, and flexible workspaces as well as the full refurbishment of the town hall building. The public space in front of the town hall was renamed Fellowship Square and a new large water feature proved immediately popular with the local community. More controversial was the demolition of the 1970s magistrate block and construction of a new civic block to accommodate council offices currently dispersed throughout the borough.

In Tower Hamlets a new town hall development scheme began in 2015 with the purchase of the eighteenth-century former Royal London Hospital site to provide the new home for all council, housing and health services, as well as meeting rooms and spaces for public use. The development forms part of the Whitechapel Vision, a large and important regeneration project to include a new life sciences campus, public spaces and new homes. A significant emphasis on environmental concerns in the municipal element includes features such as optimised water consumption and renewable energies.

The instillation of civic pride has been a recurrent theme throughout the centuries and the renovation of town halls can be crucial to civic vision. The extensive refurbishment of Liverpool Town Hall aimed to return it 'to beneficial use' while making it a 'front door' to the city, and a restoration scheme at Manchester Town Hall aimed to boost public access and ensure that the building and square retained a central role at the heart of city life. Many councils are keen to promote their former and existing municipal buildings as part of their history and heritage. Interpretation panels, audio guides, interactive information points and short films on local and town hall history are useful tools for this end, as installed at Durham Town Hall.

Town halls and adjacent public spaces are often incorporated into local cultural and seasonal events. At Waltham Forest London Borough of Culture's opening event in 2019 artists Greenaway & Greenaway presented an audio-visual film projected onto the town hall façade, telling the story of the borough with a soundtrack by musician and producer Talvin Singh in collaboration with local musicians. Barnsley Town Hall's annual Christmastime extravaganza has been a curious mix of family fun and serious council business, including live music, craft stalls, family activities and Santa's grotto, and a chance for residents to chat with councillors and ask questions about their role.

The survival of redundant town hall buildings is often dependent upon a private sector vision, and some have been saved from demolition by being repurposed, often as hotels, housing or commercial venues. Fulham's Grade II listed town hall lay derelict for a decade before restoration commenced in 2021 to convert it to a boutique hotel, event venue and coworking space with restaurants and bars. In the summer of that year the developer, in partnership with Art Below, used the building as a temporary art and exhibition space, featuring works created during lockdown by over 150 artists, with talks, live music and performances.

Multifunctional buildings at the heart of communities are becoming more commonplace, especially in smaller towns, their typically spacious premises can offer an impressive array of participatory activities, including learning spaces, community group meetings, art exhibitions and local history museums and archives. Such transformations are often only possibly with grants and funding from organisations such as the Heritage Lottery Fund, and charitable trusts are often created to manage and run arts and cultural programmes based at town halls.

Town Halls

Barnsley Town Hall was illuminated in 2017 with a light display projected on the clock face, as part of the town's Christmas extravaganza. (Jay Garrett)

Many still-functioning town halls also now operate as entertainment and function venues, the wedding market being especially lucrative, their heritage and decorative interiors being a huge draw. Others continue to provide venue space for concerts and gigs, and many town halls hold regular club or comedy nights and host theatre productions as well as seasonal events such as atmospheric candlelit carol concerts.

Whether a small market hall or part of a large civic complex, town hall buildings are as central and dominant within their settings as they ever were, forming familiar visual landmarks within their streetscapes. They are historically, socially and politically significant, reflecting the history of their town's development, as well as in charting competition between towns and, of course, are a display of local civic pride. Many have been designated as listed buildings and remain relevant to their citizens, either as a working town hall or with renewed relevance through reuse.

In 2019, Walthamstow Town Hall had a central role in Waltham Forest's London Borough of Culture celebrations. A film entitled *Into the Forest*, telling the story of the borough through the eyes of its diverse communities by artists Greenaway and Greenaway, was projected onto the façade, set to a soundtrack by Talvin Singh. (Jay Garrett)

An installation at the Art in the Age of Now exhibition, Fulham Town Hall. (Michael G. Spafford)

The 1970s Camden Town Hall annexe has been converted into a luxury hotel, modernised with a glass-heavy rooftop extension and a quirky, red 'pill-like' exterior lift. (Author's collection)

5
Town Halls and Society

Town halls provide integral functions to the societies they serve, from the practical to the pleasurable, whether as venues for voting or places to attend performances. They are so much more than places of administration, and have a long tradition of being the focus for the gathering together of local communities, often in their hundreds and thousands, for celebration and for protest. Adjacent public town squares developed from informal and often irregular marketplace layouts, and continue to be significant features in towns and cities, facilitating and promoting social life as well as being a space where people gathered to be seen or heard.

The very nature of the town hall as a political building has naturally lent itself to be the perfect venue for hosting many a political speech. Each town hall boasts of the notable politicians and prime ministers that have graced its balconies or steps, speaking to gathered crowds. The town hall has also provided a venue for citizens to be heard, and over the years all manner of things have been debated and protested at town halls throughout the country, from local issues such as rate increases, road closures and cuts to services, to national and international concerns, such as food shortages, political leadership and climate change.

Public protest became increasingly common from the sixteenth century, when changes involving redistribution of land, property, wealth and authority following the Dissolution of the Monasteries affected public life. Many towns under ecclesiastical control experienced a loss of schools and charities as well as upkeep and maintenance of roads and bridges, and

Rochdale Municipal Jubilee procession, Town Hall Square, 1906. (Postcard: author's collection)

Crowds gathered at Brighton Town Hall during the 1841 election hustings. (Royal Pavilion and Museums, Brighton and Hove)

regulation of the marketplace and other buildings, and at the same time a growing population created problems with housing and food supply, sanitation and unemployment. Concerns over tax increases, high food prices and political and religious animosity in place by the mid-seventeenth century continued into the eighteenth. These continued tensions and occasional violence periodically erupted, especially in Parliamentary elections and around polling days.

The town hall had a particularly central role in the nineteenth century, a period of widespread calls and protests for national democratic reform. New town halls were perfect forums for citizens to engage in political debate, especially as they symbolised the purpose and aspirations of both citizen and town. No town hall better represents this than Birmingham's, built when the town was at the forefront of such protests. In the twentieth century, protests at key points in time as the century progressed involved a wider cross-section of society, as the town hall continued to be a focus for community action. From Rent Acts protests early in the century to the Poll Tax protests of the early 1990s and the climate change and Black Lives Matter protests of more recent times, the spaces outside town halls have served as key meeting points prior to and at the end of protest marches, as places of demonstration, and as platforms for associated speeches by groups and individuals.

The gathering of people at town halls for celebration has been equally significant. The occasion of a new town hall, and subsequent anniversaries especially centenaries, were themselves momentous civic occasions bound up with great ceremony and celebration, both at the laying of foundation stones and grand openings, as well as subsequent anniversary celebrations. Presided over by the mayor, fellow worthies and guests of the corporation, these occasions were often attended by a visiting dignitary or member of the nobility, sometimes even royalty, as well as the architect, all preceded by a grand procession. These celebrations invariably attracted large crowds at the town hall as well as along the procession route, and commemorative medals were usually struck for the occasion. In the later nineteenth and early to mid-twentieth centuries in particular, visiting guests invited to town hall celebrations

Black Lives Matter protest outside Hackney Town Hall, summer 2020. (Ian Roberts)

would be met at the station by carriage, often accompanied to the town hall by a mounted escort or even a marching band with throngs of flag-waving townsfolk lining the streets of the route. Arrival by car and even helicopter became more usual in subsequent decades.

The town hall has a long tradition of being the focus of national celebrations, usually related to the victory and conclusion of war and associated peace, and monarch-related commemorations – birthdays, marriages, deaths and accessions to the throne. Town halls were often illuminated and decked with bunting, and would form the start or finishing point for parades and processions, sometimes culminating in speeches and a series of toasts and often accompanied by the lighting of a large bonfire in the evening.

Town halls have also been the focus for impromptu as well as organised celebrations, especially following news of the end of war hostilities. News of the end of the war with Japan in September 1945 spread quickly, and within hours people had gathered outside town halls throughout the country with impromptu parades and marches, as at South Shields, whose townsfolk gathered to listen to the Harton Colliery Band playing outside the town hall. In neighbouring Jarrow, as ships' horns and air-raid sirens signalled the news, around 3,000 people assembled at the town hall and the mayor delivered a speech from the front steps before calling for three cheers, followed by a minute's silence for the fallen.

Did You Know?

Birmingham Town Hall was designed by Joseph Aloysius Hansom, better known as the creator of the Hansom cab.

Above: The opening of Ossett Town Hall, 2 June 1908. (Postcard: author's collection)
Left: Bridlington Town Hall's opening in May 1932 was performed by the mayor with a symbolic unlocking of the new building with a golden key – the new town hall symbolised a golden period in the town's progress. (*Yorkshire Post and Leeds Intelligencer*, 12 May 1932)

The opening of Bradford's new town hall in 1873 included a revival of defunct Bishop Blaise celebrations not seen since 1825. The bishop was the patron saint of wool combing, a strong Bradford occupation, so this revival was important in fostering and celebrating town pride. (*The Illustrated London News*, Mary Evans Picture Library)

The proclamation of George V, Preston Town Hall, 9 May 1910. (Postcard: author's collection)

Leyton Town Hall decorated to commemorate Peace Day, 1919. (Postcard: author's collection)

Celebrations were often grand and bombastic affairs, with special celebration committees and funds allocated for the purpose. They were ostensibly for everyone, although attendance for most people would have been limited to gathering outside. Specific events forming part of a programme of celebrations could be more inclusive, such as meals for the unemployed or the 'less fortunate', as in 1863 when the aged poor of Wycombe were fed a meal at noon as part of the programme of events celebrating the marriage of the Prince of Wales in 1853, followed by an evening meal for more distinguished guests in the early evening. This separation of events between elements of the townsfolk, and with the more banquet-type affairs for invited guests of the mayor, was fairly common. Nevertheless, the ethos of the town coming together in celebration was an important one so that the townsfolk were not mere witnesses to the spectacle, but also participants. The pinnacle of Derby's town hall celebrations in 1780 for the birthday of George III centred around a large bonfire. Large crowds gathered before the town's mayor, worthies and regimental officers as various toasts were made to the royal family, followed by constitutional and loyal toasts, and in a magnanimous gesture the public were also given ale and wine.

Commemorations have extended to recognising people and events in a more permanent way, most notably through portraiture and sculptural depictions of local worthies, and are visual representations of local political life. Portraits and sculpture of former mayors and other worthies are displayed in prominent and important places within the town hall. Sometimes other mediums are used, as at Morley Town Hall where memorial stained-glass windows were unveiled in July 1950 in memory of Aldermen Brian Barker and Thomas Marshall.

A town hall's art and design collections are socially, culturally and historically significant, often carefully curated from the outset and so reflecting a town's status and ambition at the time of construction. Manchester's town hall collection is particularly impressive, with over 3,000 pieces of sculpture, paintings, furniture, silverware, ceramics, glass and textiles, many designed by or approved of by the building's architect, Alfred Waterhouse, to complement and enhance the architecture and design of the town hall. Commendably, the sculpture gallery has been renovated and restored to public use, and the painting collection has been digitised and can be viewed online via the Art UK website. An emblem of the city, the worker bee, is featured throughout the building, representing the city's work ethic and hive of activity, and a series of murals in the great hall depict different points in Manchester's history. Sometimes though, past choices of art and statuary can be

The entrance and Sculpture Hall to Manchester Town Hall contains busts and statues of influential Manchester-related people, including John Dalton, James Prescott Joule and John Barbirolli. (Postcard: author's collection)

problematic today, notably where individuals are connected to imperial power, subjugation of other nations and slavery. This is the case at Deptford, where art and statuary chosen for the town hall of 1905 reflected the area's maritime connections and included statues of three prominent figures, Sir Francis Drake, Admiral Robert Blake and Horatio Nelson, who were all connected with the slave trade.

Most commemorations relating to ordinary townsfolk, however, tend to be largely restricted to war memorials that remember the fallen. These are often memorial plaques in wood or stone located inside the building, although monumental memorials are sometimes located outside town halls, in prominent positions.

At Alcester it was decided that the town hall itself should became the memorial to the town's First World war dead rather than erect a new memorial. The building's freehold was obtained from George Seymour, 7th Marquess of Hertford, and it was renamed the Alcester War Memorial Town Hall. At Waltham Abbey, too, a war memorial was decided against, and instead a new hospital was constructed as a direct legacy of the town hall wartime hospital; the Waltham Abbey War Memorial Cottage Hospital opened in 1921.

The multipurpose function of the town hall extended to public entertainment, especially from the nineteenth century when purpose-built halls were increasingly incorporated into town hall design. Public music concerts, recitals and theatrical performances were a hugely important part of a town's social calendar for those who could afford to attend. Performances often formed part of regional or national musical tours, or were part of local arts programmes, while others were fundraising concerts for local causes and charities.

Above: The Hyde Town Hall memorial comprises five wall-mounted oak panels bearing the names of local men who were killed in the First World War. They were erected annually for the duration of the war. A sixth bronze panel, depicting Mayoress Evelyn Rose Welch (1914–16), was added in 1934. The mural was painted by local artist Harry Rutherford. (Gerald England)

Left: War memorial set within an exterior recess of Clydebank Town Hall. (Lairich Rig)

> # MUSIC.
>
> ON Monday next, the 2d of October, (being the Anniversary-Meeting of the County-Hospital) will be performed, at the Town-Hall, in Northampton,
>
> ## A CONCERT,
>
> Which will consist of the most favourite OVERTURES, CONCERTOS, &c.
>
> TICKETS to be had at Mr. Barrett's, Mr. Dabney's, and Mr. Burnham's, Bookseller, at 2s. 6d. each.
>
> The Doors will be opened, for the Reception of Company, at Six o'Clock; and the Concert will begin precisely at Seven.
>
> A Band will be provided for a BALL, after the Concert.

Advertisement for an upcoming concert at Northampton Town Hall. (*Northampton Mercury*, 2 October 1775)

Colchester's annual Oyster Feast is an important part of the town's history and civic calendar, and is traditionally held on the last Friday of each October. Hosted by the mayor, it is attended by dignitaries from around the country and arts and entertainment worthies. Various Colchester citizens, usually those active in local charities, civic bodies and good causes, are invited via a public lottery. (Postcard: author's collection)

In Yarmouth, a series of amateur concerts held in 1838 included the option of purchasing tickets to six performances for 'no more than a guinea', and in September 1845 a morning of Italian music was one of the events on offer at Reading Town Hall, where a 'highly fashionable and numerous attendance' was hoped for. Many working-class townsfolk would not usually have been permitted or been financially able to attend town hall events. In 1844, a fancy dress fundraising ball for over 1,200 guests was held at Liverpool Town Hall's ballroom suite, and although hundreds of people gathered to watch the guests arrive they were financially excluded from the event itself. Even if affordability was not an issue, the late times of these events (the merriment at Liverpool ended at 5 a.m.) was another barrier to working-class folk who would have had to rise early for work.

In the twentieth century all types of performances became more affordable and accessible to more people, as disposable incomes extended to wider section of society. Performances have ranged from professional concerts to gigs and pantomime, as well as local theatrical productions. Wrestling and boxing tournaments were also popular events, especially in the mid- to late twentieth century, and drew huge crowds.

Use of town halls by individuals and groups has a long tradition, sometimes for rather niche events, other times with a more universal appeal. In the 1770s Mr Wall Du Val of London's Hatton Garden opened a dancing and fencing school at Lynn Town Hall. Many town halls have

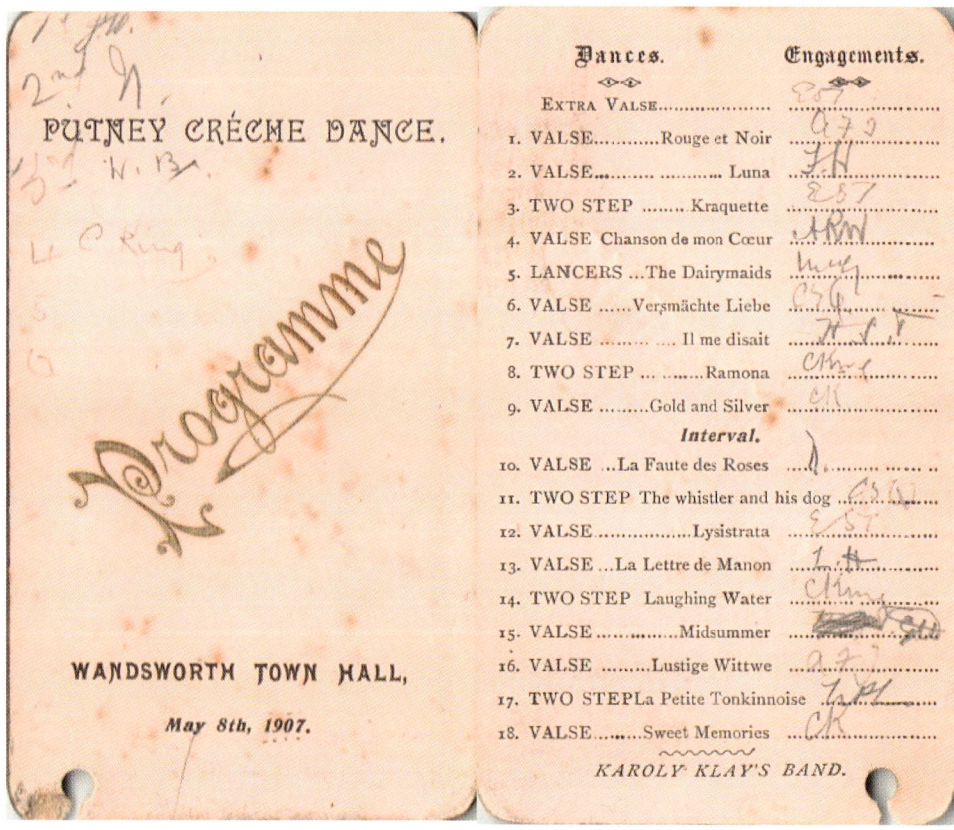

Dance card for the Putney Creche Dance at Wandsworth Town Hall, 8 May 1907. (Author's collection)

Gig at Oxford Town Hall, 2014. (Yves Maurer)

also been used as venues for sales and auctions over the years, as at Sheffield as far back as the 1740s. In summer 1786, Wokingham Town Hall was used by the landlord of a local hostelry as a venue for a singing competition, with prizes of a silver punch ladle and a silver cup. Curiously, entries were only permitted by people who dined at his hostelry, but only if they were not Wokingham residents. Over the years shows and competitions continued to be held at various town halls, as at Evesham Town Hall, which hosted the Chrysanthemum and Vegetable Show early in the twentieth century, and again when it was revived some forty years or so later, in 1947. Wider community use of the town hall became more common from the twentieth century, including plays and pantomimes staged by local amateur theatre groups and various community programmes, as at Forres Town Hall, which has hosted a varied programme over the years, including a playgroup, coffee mornings, exercise class and pop-up shops.

Redundant town halls often continue to serve their local communities. Schemes such as Skipton Town Hall's renovation and redevelopment as a community hub and home of Craven Museum and Exhibition Gallery was highly successful. The scheme involved the community throughout the process, and the renovated venue opened following a 2017 public consultation on plans for design and interpretation. In 2018, a Resilient Heritage Fund project laid the foundations for a transformation of Kidderminster Town Hall into a community and arts facility for the townspeople, including opening up access to the building's historic spaces. Trowbridge's town hall building is another successful venture with the community at its heart. In 2012, a trust was formed to secure the building's long-term future 'to continue to benefit the people of Trowbridge'. As a community-owned and -led charity, it houses a café, boutiques, live music, cinema and creative studios, as well as hosting a range of leisure activities. Their website declares that their past inspires them, with their role being to bring people together and empower them. It includes a statement that could be applied to town halls everywhere: 'This is your town hall. Come and join us.'

Above left: Poster advertising wrestling events at Leeds Town Hall, 1988. (Author's collection)

Above right: Poster for Skipton Town Hall's 2019 Big Community Doodle, part of its successful community event The Big Draw. The town hall is home to Craven Museum and Exhibition Gallery, a concert hall and visitor and information centre, and has been especially successful as a place for community-centered projects and events. (Skipton Town Hall)

Kidderminster Town Hall. (Jacqueline Bryan)

What Next?

Visit
Some areas within town halls are public spaces that may be visited during normal opening hours. Art and sculpture are often on public display, and there may be occasional exhibitions. However, access to some areas may be restricted or only be open at certain dates and times. Many town halls offer guided or self-guided heritage tours. Check your local town hall website for access arrangements and for details of any tours.

Read
There are several publications covering various aspects of town halls, including architecture, history and politics, and they range from simple introductory booklets to more scholarly works. A selection of these are listed below:

Calveley Cotton, A., *Town Halls* (1936) – A useful reference guide to the planning of interwar town halls and civic centres.

Cunningham, J., *Victorian and Edwardian Town Halls* (1981) – A weighty but interesting tome on the town halls of this period.

Read Me Series, *Town Halls, Guildhalls and Market Halls* (1973) – A basic and simple introduction to the building type, in the form of a thirty-five-page booklet.

Reeves, D. (ed.), *Town Hall: Buildings, People and Power* (2018) – 'Written by people who care about design and democracy, and the people who work in these amazing buildings.' This is a wonderful collection of photographs and stories relating to all aspects of town halls.

Stewart, J., *Twentieth Century Town Halls: Architecture of Democracy* (2019) – This book looks at town halls in a worldwide context, with a brief history of the building type and a selection of case studies.

Tittler, R., *Architecture and Power: The Town Hall and the English Urban Community c. 1500–1640* (1991) – More academic in tone, this is an excellent publication for anyone interested in the development of the English town and governance.

Royal Commission on the Ancient and Historical Monuments of Scotland, *Tolbooths and Townhouses: Civic Architecture in Scotland to 1833* (1996) – This provides an excellent in-depth look at their development, including accounts of surviving examples as well as those that have been demolished or altered.

Many town halls and former town halls have potted histories available online, either on their own websites or within the websites of local history societies. Some town hall histories have been produced in book form, including A. Wilkins & P. McIntosh, *West Bromwich Town Hall* (2003); L. Johnson, *Frome Town Hall* (2017); and A. Pevers, *Birmingham Town Hall: An Architectural History* (2003). The intriguingly titled *Kirton Town Hall Recipe Book* (2011) is also worth a mention.

John Boughton's fabulous blog Municipal Dreams contains entries on town halls, including accounts of town halls participating in Open House London: municipaldreams.wordpress.com.

Support
If your local town hall building is earmarked for development or demolition, find out what the plans are from your local council. If this negatively impacts local heritage, start or join a campaign to raise awareness.